Night Moves in Ohio

poems by

William Heath

Finishing Line Press
Georgetown, Kentucky

Night Moves in Ohio

To my sister, Alice Marie Baker, for sharing those years growing up in Poland and so much more, and to Joel Beeghly, Terry Mort, Jim Lewis, Dave Osborn, and the Lee Run Road crew, as well as the class of 1960 at Poland Seminary High. Too many are too soon gone, including Jim Glaser, Butch Talbott, and Hank Litler, to whom I can no longer pass the baton on our 440-yard relay team.

Copyright © 2019 by William Heath
ISBN 978-1-64662-048-7 First Edition
All rights reserved under International and Pan-American Copyright Conventions. No part of this book may be reproduced in any manner whatsoever without written permission from the publisher, except in the case of brief quotations embodied in critical articles and reviews.

ACKNOWLEDGMENTS

"Night Moves in Ohio," *Poetry Now*
"The Six-Shooter Survived the West," *handsel*
"Nightwatch," *approaches*
"How I Left the War and Took Up Basketball," *Mid-Atlantic Review*

This is a work of poetry not history; names, places, and dates may not be reliable.

Publisher: Leah Maines
Editor: Christen Kincaid
Cover Art: William Heath
Author Photo: Joseph Caminals
Cover Design: Elizabeth Maines McCleavy

Printed in the USA on acid-free paper.
Order online: www.finishinglinepress.com
also available on amazon.com

Author inquiries and mail orders:
Finishing Line Press
P. O. Box 1626
Georgetown, Kentucky 40324
U. S. A.

Table of Contents

Steel Valley Elegy 1

My Father Put the Shot 3

Our Black Sheep 5

The Saywell Side 6

Recess on the Poland Playground 7

Kissing Games in Ohio 8

Skipping Stones 9

How I Left the War and Took up Basketball 10

Paperboy 11

Knife Fights 12

A Hit in Shaker Heights 13

High Jumper 14

I Beat Dolph 15

Typing Class 17

Sock Hop 18

The Six-Shooter Survived the West 19

The Green Man 20

Night Moves in Ohio 21

The Girls from Campbell 22

An Inside Job 23

Guts and Glory 25

Pledge Night 26

Nightwatch 28

Assassinating Nixon 29

Milking Time 31

Mom's Final Days 33

The Raft 35

The Long-Distance Seer 36

Steel Valley Elegy

I speak Steel Valley American. Once mills
lined the Mahoning River from Youngstown
Sheet and Tube's Jeannette Blast Furnace
on Brier Hill to Republic Steel in Struthers.
Coal intensified to coke turned iron ore
into molten ingots that were rolled into slabs,
scarfed free of impurities, shaped for strength:
bridges to span waters, girders for skyscrapers,
tanks, ships, guns, and shells to win World War II,
machines and factories for our bounty.

The workers—Honkies from Smokey Hollow,
Slovaks from Nebo, Dagos, Polacks, Blacks—
dressed for combat: hard hats, safety glasses,
asbestos coats, steel-toed boots. Beware
of breathing tainted air. Open hearth blast
furnaces singed eyebrows, seared lungs, "pants
on fire" no metaphor. At the last whistle
dehydrated men headed for the taverns
on tap at each plant gate, downed boilermakers
(a shot of whiskey dropped in a mug of beer),
cashed checks, played the "bug," staggered home.

Men made serious money making steel.
A house with a lawn, a Ford or Chevy
in the drive. Soot on windows meant food
on the table. Mills created the weather:
skies dark in daytime, bright at night; clothes
hung in the cellar to avoid black rain.
The city was called "Little Chicago,"
seventy-five bombings—"Youngstown tune-ups"—
as Cleveland and Pittsburgh mobsters blew
each other apart for control of the bug
and other games of chance. Barbers charged
five bucks for a haircut, ten to start your car.

Crossing the bridge into town I saw
the Valley of Ashes in *The Great Gatsby*:
grey heaps of slag, bins of scrap metal,
the fuming rusty-orange sulfurous river
that might ignite at the flip of a match;

low, corrugated buildings topped by tall
towers and vent stacks burning off waste gas;
serpentine trains shunted into sideyards,
scotched into freight cars, unloaded one by one.

My Czech girlfriend, whose father worked in steel,
spread a blanket in her backyard above the valley.
As evening fell the infernal glow of the mills
became magical. Yellow flames from smelters
made air-borne soot sparkle, blotting out the stars.
White-hot slabs glided down conveyor belts.
The screeching, clanging industrial din
had a percussive rhythm. Teens in love,
for all we knew our kisses lasted hours.
Now the mills are gone. The only people left
misplaced their car keys—still I celebrate
the steel valley's brutal lost beauty.

My Father Put the Shot

In the photo he stands
in track shorts and top,
hands clasped behind his back
to accentuate his biceps.
The "O" on his broad chest
proof he put the shot
for the Oberlin track team.
A farmer's son, he worked
hard as a boy, putting
the shot just one more
form of tossing rocks out
of a ploughed corn field.

After graduation he taught
chemistry in a rural school.
He loved to tell the tale of how
a bully ignored his order
to leave the class, gripping
his desk screwed to the floor.
My father jerked the desk
into the air, tossed it
and the bully out the door.
The next day the lad came back
with his much larger father.

"Did you throw my boy out of class?"
he demanded. Dad replied,
"Yes, I did." "Did he deserve it?"
"Yes, he did." "Well, if he acts up
again, beat the hell out of him,"
he said, shaking Dad's hand,
smacking his son on the head
for good measure. Feats like these
get a man promoted to principal.
His office at Hays Junior High
in Youngstown had a drawer full
of confiscated weapons—switch
blades, clubs, even a zip gun
wrapped in black tape.

He enforced discipline by swats
with a perforated paddle hung
on the wall behind his desk.
Perhaps that's why he only hit
me twice in his life—once for
filching a neighbor boy's toy
truck and bulldozer, then
for faking a bicycle accident
beside the highway, enhanced
by my ketchup-covered body.
He used his belt and, his voice
breaking, admonished, "Don't ever
make me have to do that again."

Our Black Sheep

Uncle Frank, grandfather's brother,
at fourteen served twenty days
in the county jail for stealing
another kid's pair of ice skates—
it wasn't his first offense—
at twenty-one he did hard time
for filching a pack of skunk skins.
Once near Oberlin he fell into a stupor
at an Erie Lackawanna line crossing.
The speeding train, no time to toot,
whisked his horse to greener pastures,
leaving Frank and buggy unscathed.
Deaf to his mother's pleas he played
his favorite, "All By Myself," endlessly
on the Victrola. One drunken night
driving home in his Model T Ford,
he sheered off three telephone poles,
finally stopped by smacking the side
of the house. Next morning my dad
went out to inspect the damage.
The poles, cut away at ground level,
still dangled from sagging wires.
Each severed pole had swung up,
clearing the way for the car
to hit the next. Everyone agreed
Uncle Frank led a charmed life,
until his liver gave out. Dad,
who never touched a drop of
the creature, helped carry the coffin.
They buried Frank on Butternut Ridge,
yonder from grandfather's farm.

The Saywell Side

Mom's parents wouldn't let Dad
stay in the house, lacking cash
for a hotel, he slept on the floor

of a laundry room at the back,
snuck out before dawn to avoid
running into Mom's mother.

George Saywell fancied himself
upper crust, but after the Great
Crash he couldn't wing it, never

invited his high-toned friends
to their home in Hudson,
calling it "a miserable hovel."

Every Sunday he went golfing.
Mom's mom, in an early photo
with her sisters, looks pensive.

Nobody knew for sure what killed
Fanny's spirit. She became colorless.
dressed drably, was an inept cook,

detested meat. She wore her hair
in a plain bun, took little interest
in anything, stayed in her room.

She never allowed her daughter
in the kitchen, so when Mom
married Dad she couldn't cook.

When Fanny's mind and body
worsened, to pay for her final care
George had to sell the house.

Recess on the Poland Playground

Bill Hallock hits a long fly ball,
Terry Mort, giving chase, runs
nose first into an oak tree.
Under the sliding board
Billy Heath sends Jethro down
to the high jump pit to tell
Helen Buddie he loves her.
Behind the backstop Debi
lowers her shorts, only lets
Jimmy Lewis look. He bends over,
peeks, runs off, puzzled.
As Larry Hancock is telling
Billy the school janitor heads
a gang of rustlers, Jethro reports
Helen thinks Billy is a sissy.
Then Sidney Owens, eager to begin
necking at age eight, tackles Billy—
he squirms free, mounts his bike
from behind, rides out of danger.
Back in class the diminutive teacher,
Midget Auto Racer, climbs
a chair to clean the blackboard,
while Paul Williams and Kathy Justice
play kissy-face in the coat closet.
When school lets out, Larry
leads Billy, Joel, Jethro, Jimmy, Terry,
and Paul down to Yellow Creek,
shows them a sealed tunnel—
part of the underground railroad
once used by slaves to slip away
from the old town tavern—
now the rustlers' secret hangout.
They squint into an inch-wide crack
between two cement blocks,
a flashlight probes nothing
but blackness. They hear the drip,
drip, drip of falling water. Larry
is sure it's the clop, clop, clop
of horses' hooves—rustlers! They
get the hell of there, outracing
horse thieves all the way home.

Kissing Games in Ohio

It started in third grade. Girls
chased boys on the playground,
kissed whoever they caught.
By junior high we graduated
to Spin the Bottle. Down
in Wendy's basement
Rec room we sat in a circle,
a Coke bottle in the center,
taking turns. The spin
decided who was kissed.
Then came Post Office,
more privacy, freedom to select.
The postmaster announced
a letter, before delivery
postage paid in the next room.
If the transaction lingered,
loud protests and doors,
locked or not, thrown open.
At last Flashlight in the dark,
any couple caught by the beam
not kissing got the flashlight
that finally was killed. I recall
pitch-black wandering,
kissing some plum-luscious
lips. We were speaking
in tongues so to speak. I
never learned whose lips
I tasted. Sophomore year
all kissing games ceased, no
more sharing, we paired off,
couples, parked by the lake
to watch "submarine races,"
now held exclusive rights
to their precious kisses.

Skipping Stones

What boy, with a stream
pooling nearby to form
a neat swimming hole,
didn't? The trick was
smooth flat ones, circular
to fit the curve of an index
finger. A sidearm toss
with a final flick of the wrist
gave the stone the proper
spin to skim the surface,
and skip, skip, skip, skip again
before it suddenly sank.
It took a keen eye to spot
the best prospects, strength
and skill for a perfect throw,
and then, by god, the stone
took on a grace, a kind of joy
as each airborne leap broke
free of the law of gravity
to fly for a moment—until
the water claimed its own.

How I Left the War and Took Up Basketball

The first time he whipped
a behind-the-back pass
to the open man on his blind side
Bob Cousy knew he was a star.
A small man with big hands
quick as a poet his pin-
point passes scored baskets.

Me, I practiced
down in our pitch-black
cement cellar, dribbling
with either hand in the dark.
Sometimes I sat with my eyes shut,
spinning the ball on my fingers,
rubbing the nubbles
and whispering to myself.

This was near the end
of the Ohio phase of the Korean War
when coming home at dusk
from the battle of Hidden Valley
and Lee Run Creek
I ran head-first into a barbed wire fence
slicing my skin at the hair line.
My mother screamed to see
the web of blood
while I searched my skull in the mirror
praying for a scar.

At first I shot
from the hip, pushing off
on my left leg to launch
a giant step up
with my right, banking
the ball off the board
to drop through the hoop.
By junior high I had
a fall-away jump shot
and basketballs
on the brain.

Paperboy

My predecessor coasted
too fast down a driveway
and out onto the road
where a speeding car
took his life. His body
was gone by the time
I got there but I saw
the blood on his bike,
front wheel spinning,
papers strewn in a ditch,
one shoe. Nonetheless
I took the job, the pay
wasn't much, I hated
getting up so early,
some houses had dogs
snapping at my legs,
yet I had fringe benefits.

Squeezing a pair of plyers
from my back pocket
the wire girding the stack
snaps back and the papers
fluff up as if in relief.
I pack them best I can
in my handlebar basket,
peddle off on my route
that always featured
the thirty-something lady—
lustrous hair piled high,
diaphanous pink negligee,
Janet-Leigh-like shape—
greeting me each morning
on her front porch.
I suppose, I guess,
as I would have said
back then, the offer
was there, but I was
just a boy, mumbling
in reply to her thanks,
"You're welcome, Mam."

Knife Fights

At Boy Scout camp my idea
of a good prank was to tie
Jim Lewis's shoelaces to
the frame of the top bunk
and see what happened
when he jumped off.
As was only right in
a just world, my reward
a richly deserved fist
in the face, a fat lip.
Usually, though, when we
fought at home, our practice
was to snatch carving knives
from a handy rack and circle
the kitchen table making
wicked swipes in the air
to the tune of cuss-laden threats.
Not a good idea, I admit.
But inevitably we burst
into savage laughter
as only friendly rivals can.

A Hit in Shaker Heights
October 30, 1959

I was seventeen, visiting
my cousin in Shaker Heights, posh
suburb of Cleveland where bad things
rarely happen. On Scottsdale Boulevard
a yellow sash across a driveway, boys
being boys we wanted to know what
the fuss was about. Between the garage
and the house a pool of blood, chalk
outlines of a body, a gun, a knife.
A woman came with a garden hose,
washed the blood down a drain.

I was from Poland, suburb of mobbed-up
Youngstown, that juicy bone of contention
between Cleveland and Pittsburgh for control
of vending machines, juke boxes, the bug,
gambling, prostitution, hard drugs.
Bombings were commonplace, murders
no rarity. This, my first crime scene.
Mike Sperazzo was shot from ambush.
He'd done time for armed robbery, fencing
stolen property; he was a bookie,
played the horses, bank-rolled floating
crap games. Maybe the hit was to settle
a score, or a mob boss gave the word.

What haunts me is that his wife
heard the car pull in, out the window
saw a man by the hedge fire twice,
slip away, return. The killer stepped
on Mike's chest for the coup de grâce.
Did she rush out of the house to see
if he was dead, then call the police?
When we arrived, cop cars and reporters
were gone. She was alone in the house,
a Mafia wife who hosed her husband's
blood, pooled beside the chalk outline
of his body, down the driveway drain.

High Jumper

I place black tape
on my bedroom wall
at six-feet, my height,
for hours I imagine
if it were a crossbar
how I could clear it.
I am a high jumper
with a tell-tale
bounce in my stride
and in those days
a leap like that breaks
the school record.
The Western Roll
is my style, first
a giant kick up
with my right leg,
a quick mid-air twist
to place my belly
above the bar,
then a backwards kick
with my left leg
before I smack down
in the sawdust pit
and look up to see
the jump is mine.

I Beat Dolph

Dolph Shayes's basketball camp
was in the Upper Adirondacks
near Plattsburg, New York.
The summer before my senior year
I went there for two weeks.
The best foul shooter in
the NBA, his long set shot,
well before the three-point rule,
a lethal wonder. He took fifty
foul shots each week, swishing
at least 45. Top that and you got
a red patch with white letters,
"I Beat Dolph." Third time around
I hit 47, claimed my reward.

Each cabin formed a team
in an on-going tournament.
Our tallest player Tommy Piper,
heir to the Piper Cub we all
longed to fly one wealthy day.
A point guard, the offense flowed
through me, but in the first half
of the championship game,
I was ejected for five fouls.
Weeping tears of baffled rage
I stomped off the court, certain
I had cost my guys the trophy
we were sure we'd win. Instead
of sitting on the bench I ran
to the woods, circled the lake,
came back to my cabin at dusk.
Coach, waiting on my bunk,
said he was ashamed of me,

I should have stayed, rooted
for our players, who,
to my astonishment, won
without me. Next day Dolph
reminded me that basketball
was a team game. A point guard
should know that. I was blinded,

not the last time, by my ego.
I was not indispensable.

My coach, I learned, during
the 1950s point-fixing scandal,
took the fall for CCNY's famous
head coach, lost his career.
Dolph knew the true story,
hired him for his camp.
He taught me good sportsmanship,
and the topsy-turvy way
a gentleman folds his pants:
first align the cuffs, then
slide them on the hanger.

Typing Class

On a senior lark Jethro and I
took typing. The other students,
prepping to be secretaries,
intent on learning to type
fast and error-free while we
horsed around, slam-banging
through speed tests, racking up
so many typos the teacher shook
her head, declared us hopeless.
I laughed loudly when Jethro,
crumpling another botched sheet,
hissed, "Out damn spot!" an allusion
everyone else missed. I can still
hear our teacher, in her throaty
Alabama drawl: "Now class make
a five-space indention," glance
at the clock, and say, "Ready.
Go." She, after all these years,
taught me an essential skill.
My thanks come too late,
Miss Ritz, but without you
I couldn't type these words.

Sock Hop

They swayed like roadside grass
after the truck passes,
waved seaweed arms
like a drowning man.
In unison they stamped out
some unseen fire.
But there was no band
on the stage that banked
one end of the basketball court
whose sharp-edged wall cut
Doug Hill off at the hip
after he hit a driving lay-up.
The speakers made no sound.
No turntables turned.
No penny loafers
scattered by the Exits,
no socks buffing
the scuffed-up floor,
no final score boasted of
one more home town victory
in electric dots.

The Six-Shooter Survived the West

obscenely
like the stripper
at Geneva-on-the-Lake
in fringed G-string, tasseled pasties,
who used one in lieu
of another weapon,
thus triggering the crowd
to shoot off its mouth.

That recalls
the time we guys
sneaked squirt guns
into the Youngstown
house of burlesque.
Between acts we
positioned ourselves near
the front-row strokers
to get in range.
How proper it was
that every time she'd hiss
and squat and bare
her shaven twat we
shot straight. Why
masturbate
given such power?

The Green Man
"Print the legend"

As a boy he climbed up
a utility pole to retrieve
a bird's nest. He heard
the hot lines singing
before his face brushed
high tension and the shock
melted it. The one eye
that survived slid down
a pink cheek. The full nose
drained to small red holes.
His mouth was a black
breathing scar. Too sensitive
to ever see the sun again,
at night the Green Man
walked the back roads
of western Pennsylvania
between New Galilee
and Kopple until the word
spread. One summer night
we packed six in a car
to catch a glimpse of that
incredible face in the full glare
of our headlights. The sight
was electrifying. On cue,
the girls screamed in terror,
we kissed away their fear.
The cops, true to custom,
quickly pounced on
the anticipated U-turn.
They flashed us down, beams
stabbed startled faces.
We followed them to a house,
waiting for the sun to rise
so the Justice of the Peace
could impose a handsome fine
to support the town. Warned
and released we raced back
to Poland, Ohio, talking much
louder than usual, trying
to laugh away that face.

Night Moves in Ohio

A blow-job at the drive-in,
an empty bottle of Deep
Ruby Fruity Native tossed
in the back seat, so drunk
they drove off forgetting
to replace the speaker.
When it ripped out, both
giggled and he stepped
on the gas, knocking
the attendant on his ass,
splattering gravel to the highway,
peeling rubber twenty feet
down the road, heading
for the strip-mine quarries
to shake off the cops.

Still giggling they fumbled
off their clothes: he trying
to bite her bra in two,
she squeezing his nuts.
Stripped to the buff they
stumbled down to the water
and went skinny dipping,
laughing so hard they damn
near swallowed the pond.
Nobody drowned. A few years
later he came home from college,
she was a social worker.
They went parking but he
couldn't get it up when she
went down on him. Furious,
she tore off and totaled
her Chevy in a ditch.

Girls from Campbell

No sooner do we unload
the cars and select our beds
at the Lake Erie summer cottage
we seniors rented for a week
than the girls from Campbell
barge in the door, wearing
tight T-shirts and short shorts,
go straight to the fridge,
pop tops, start chugging.
One girl asks where we live.
When I say "Poland" she shakes
a wrist to show how rich we are.
Campbell for us conjures up
steel mills along the Mahoning,
the all-black basketball team
we beat in the tournament,
shady dealings of the Mafiosi
operating out of Youngstown.

A few beer cases later. One of
the Campbell girls passes out
in the bedroom while necking
with Bob, who, when he notices
no response, asks for our help.
What to do? We splash water
on her face, walk her around
the room, but all she mumbles,
repeatedly, is "Fuck Butchy,"
her no good boyfriend we're told.
At this point it's past midnight,
the problem: how to sneak
the plastered girl past the chaperone
asleep on a couch. Our solution:
carry her to their cabin, slide her
in a back bedroom window,
the only sound her Butchy mantra.
When we awake the next morning
the girls from Campbell are gone,
our fridge is bare. Perhaps
there's a moral here, but it
eludes the guys from Poland.

An Inside Job

For three summers I sold
bait, boats, fishing permits
at Evans Lake to any
lunatics who showed up
before dawn to hook their fill
of perch, bass, bluegills.
A few blacks came by to gig
for carp along the shore line
while most men wanted
to be out on the water—
fine with me, I was free
to read a good book by lunch
when the fishermen docked,
drove off with their catch.

One morning, I was late
as usual, cars lined up,
men hands on hips
scowling as I unlocked
the gate—but the back door
was open, so was the safe:
Someone, during the night,
robbed the boathouse.
The detective, decked out
in a TV trench coat, asked
a few questions, paced back
and forth, caught my eye.
"Looks like an inside job."
A lie detector would tell.

Headquarters, in Youngstown,
where the usual suspects
were wiseguys implicated
in gangland bombings. I sat
in a third floor room below
a bare bulb—a strap
across my chest, fingers
attached, the questioning
began. Yes or no my options,
I affirmed my name, address,
denied I robbed the safe,

knew about the theft.
At the end, a dim smile
for my inquisitor, I asked
how I'd done. "Not very good,
Bill." He showed me
the zig-zagging printout
proclaiming my guilt.

"Either you did this or you
know who did" I was told.
"We have your address.
You'll be hearing from us."
For weeks I rarely slept.
The crime remained unsolved.
All these years I've pondered
why my doorbell never rang.
The city cops were swamped,
or snug in the mob's pocket,
no bombers went on trial.

Why did I fail the test?
When Keats saw a sparrow
pecking the gravel he became
that bird, felt its satisfaction.
A crowbar for the door,
sensitive fingers cracked
the safe, loot crammed in a bag,
I made a clean getaway.
In my defense I plead poetry.

Guts and Glory

You bet I've got guts, I survived
high school for Christ's sake.
I wouldn't let them push me off
the high board or chug a case
of Rolling Rock, let alone smoke
one more joint, my scalp tingling
enough as it was. In spite of guys
egging me on from the back seat
I never went over the speed limit
by more than twenty miles—when
a cop pulled me over it was for
running a stop sign I never saw.
I needed glasses. I learned that
at my Vietnam draft physical.
As I stood in my underwear,
a stern-faced soldier told me to look
at the screen, state what I saw.
I spoke not a word. "Speak up,"
he snapped. "Cat got your tongue?
Tell me what you see, God damn it?"
"I'm waiting," my near-sighted
reply, "for the machine to focus."

Pledge Night
for Rich Pejeau

We thought of everything.
Ramshackle abandoned house
lost in undergrowth, rumor

had it that a couple had died
in a car crash, no relatives,
everything just as it was

when they left. Dirty dishes
in the sink, beds unmade,
stench from the garbage like

you wouldn't believe. Careful
to preserve the cobwebs, strings
tied to doors that creaked,

someone in hiding to ping
the piano when the time
came. Best of all a preserved

head stolen from science lab
prominent on the pillow,
blankets shaped like a body

under the bedspread. Blind-
folded pledges driven around,
snuck in the back to the cellar—

that was the plan. We chose Rich
to be our test case, gave him
a tiny flashlight, told him there

was something in the bedroom
we wanted him to go see.
We were sure we could smell

his fear. Reluctantly he went
up the stairs, on the first floor
the piano pinged on schedule,

a door creaked, a cobweb
brushed across his eyes,
the wind whistled through

a window open a crack.
On the second floor, he
stepped into the dark room,

his pencil-thin light shone
on the bed—gray strands of hair
on the pillow, the ghoulish

face drained of flesh, eyes like
dried raisins, yellow teeth
in a wide mirthless grin—

and said, "Oh, Hello."

Nightwatch
Lexington, Kentucky, 1972

Blackbirds clot
at the top of the tree
bare beneath a pale moon
that breaks in half
and swims through
a dark sea of clouds.
Have I mentioned
a strong night wind
whistling down
desolate streets?
The cries of those birds
mastering the air?
How we looked up,
standing on Cheapside,
beside the ominous Gothic
stone courthouse
and found ourselves lost
in a de Chirico landscape.
under an El Greco sky,
lonely and modern?

Assassinating Nixon
17 March 1971

My chance came at the burial
of Whitney Young, Lexington's
native son, who as leader of
the Urban League sometimes
supported the president.
That's why Nixon came—I
went to check out Tricky Dick.
Although the sun was shining
I noticed several tall men
in raincoats surreptitiously
whispering to their lapels
as they sidled closer to me.

In those carnivalesque days
I was a college professor
who dressed as a hippie—
beaded headband, hair
down to my shoulders,
a Fu Manchu mustache,
and a puffy-sleeved shirt
of many colors—signifying,
I later realized, I must be
a suspect character. I was
positioned a few feet away
when the limos arrived.

Nixon popped out, madly
grinning, waving his arms
in the air as if the pit pat
of applause he received
equaled an ovation. What
struck me most was his
outsized head, how thickly
his makeup was layered on.
He looked unreal, a manikin,
and yes if I had had a pistol
I could easily have shot him.

What I learned later was
that someone *had* threatened
Nixon's life. That's why
secret servicemen comprised
half the crowd, why they
pinpointed me as a person
of interest. Later his family,
informed Young's resting place
was in a segregated part
of Lexington's cemetery,
reburied him in New York.

Milking Time

Like his father beside him,
Dad straddled a one-legged stool,
left knee inside the cow's

right hind leg, zinc pail between
his knees, wary of a quick kick
spilling milk or bruising a shin.

Sometimes a sudden swish
of her tail to ward off flies
wrapped around his neck,

coarse hairs stinging his face.
Though given only easy milkers,
a Holstein with large teats took

both strong hands for results.
A good cow could fill a pail,
plus free squirts for the eager

cat at his feet. Dad liked
the taste of fresh buttermilk
surfaced with floating globules.

By age twelve he was churning,
raising and lowering a plunger
into cream to agitate it—

a tedious task that took
a long arm-aching time,
a splashing sound meant

the cream had finally broken.
The prized reward: bread,
freshly baked, a clotted cream

spread, a sprinkle of sugar.
When Dad was in his eighties
my wife Roser and I visited

his Florida double-wide,
she heard him wandering about
in the middle of the night,

found him at the refrigerator
putting butter on bread,
drinking milk from a bottle.

"Don't ever get old," he said.
"I used to do this as a boy.
It helps me sleep."

Mom's Final Days

"Ralph, I know you work hard,
but you're not a very good farmer."
"I'm not Dad, Mom. Dad's dead.
I'm a college teacher." "Farming
just doesn't pay nowadays. I think
you better quit." "Whatever
you say, Mom." "We've had
quite a dinner this evening.
People from both North and South
were there, but the Southerners
weren't very happy. The war
isn't going very well for them.
I was pleasantly surprised that
they didn't speak as badly as I
thought they would. Very little
slurring of words. Most of them
spoke proper English, so that's
something." "Who do you think
will win the war, Mom?" "Well,
that's a good question, it's touch
and go right now. It snowed
last night and I hope mother
doesn't slip on the ice." "She's
been dead a long time, Mom."
"My sister, Marie, is going to be
a nurse; my father is a patent
attorney. I think he likes me
better than mother, because he
takes me places. She lives in
the attic and never comes down."

"There's a lot of movement here
today. Some people are going
to New York and others returning
to their country of origin—I don't
know what that is, but I'm sure
the captain of the ship." "You're
in Ohio, Mom." "…has a list,
because he needs to control
the people who come on board.
I'm sure everything will settle down

once the ship has sailed. I'll be glad
to go. I would never send my child
here, it is a very sad place. They
come in and pour water on me,
and laugh about it, as if it were
a joke." "Who does that, Mom?"
"The girls who work here. They
wake me up and pour water
on me." "You mean a shower?"
"Well, you might call it that.
It isn't very scientific. They just
pour water on my head and laugh
about it. It's very sad. I'll be
glad when I get out of here
and go home." "How often
do you have a shower, Mom?"
"Once every few weeks, because
I'm going to marry an officer."

The last time I called Mom said,
"I'm awfully glad to hear from you,
we've just landed and I don't
know anybody." "Landed in what,
Mom?" "It was a flying saucer,
I believe, I can see it parked out
my window. We had a pleasant
flight. Lafayette we are here
for quite a while, so I hope they
take care of us. I don't know what
to expect here, but I'll try to keep
in touch with you, bye-bye."

Mom died in her sleep
on August 7th, 2006. Her funeral
at her childhood home of Hudson,
Ohio, was attended by a few
friends and family, as well as
a doe and two fawns.

The Raft

Drifting down the river
the stream moves so slowly
I can see each flower
if I'm looking closely.

Instead I waste my time,
half asleep, half awake,
noting only the slime
curdled along the bank.

When the water widens
into a placid lake
it seems that all movement
stops, but that's a mistake.

Remorselessly the stream
rolls on, from slow to fast,
as next white-water rapids
sweep me perilously past

treacherous rocks. Steep falls
drop abruptly to deep
turbulent pools that swirl
until I cannot keep

my balance. And so it
goes, as hours, days, years pass.
I now know with regret
that not one life will last.

The Long Distance Seer

If I die
at a rotten
old age
destroy
this poem

but if I die
of a heart attack
if like my grandfather
my heart
stops
as I am driving a fast car
or if
in a lover's arms
my heart bursts
smilingly
or if
after a hard game
of basketball
my heart beats
itself to death

publish
this prophecy
to the world.

www.ingramcontent.com/pod-product-compliance
Lightning Source LLC
LaVergne TN
LVHW041556070426
835507LV00011B/1115